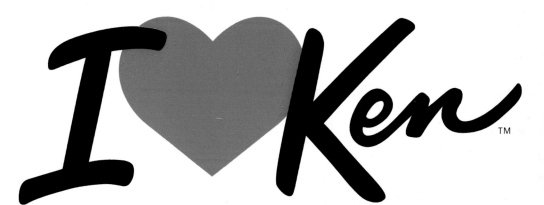

I ♥ Ken™

MY LIFE AS THE

ULTIMATE

BOYFRIEND

RUNNING PRESS
PHILADELPHIA · LONDON

9 8 7 6 5 4 3 2 1
Digit on the right indicates the number of this printing
Library of Congress Control Number: 2010933194

ISBN 978-0-7624-3939-3

Design: Gabriel Stromberg
Editorial: Kjersti Egerdahl
Image Research: Jessica Eskelsen
Production Coordination: Tom Miller
Licensing Acquisition: Josh Anderson
I ❤ Ken is produced by becker&mayer!, Bellevue, Washington.
www.beckermayer.com

Running Press Book Publishers
2300 Chestnut Street
Philadelphia, PA 19103-4371

Visit us on the web!
www.runningpress.com

Dolls on pages 39, 53 (left), 54, 55 (left), 72, 74, and 76 (outer flap) are courtesy of Jef Beck, photos by Jessica Eskelsen. All other images and illustrations are courtesy of Mattel, Inc., used with permission.

I ♥ Ken™

MY LIFE AS THE ULTIMATE BOYFRIEND

as told to Jef Beck

Contents

When it comes to knowing a thing or two about the "Ultimate Boyfriend," I'm pretty much an expert. I was smitten with Ken from day one. We're probably the only couple in history to have dated on and off for fifty years! (Though I wouldn't recommend this—our situation is definitely unique.) We almost made it down the aisle a dozen or so times but somehow didn't quite get to the "I do's." (But I'm *so* not complaining. Look at all the beautiful dresses I got to wear!)

People think they know Ken because of his public persona. What they don't know is that Ken may be handsome on the outside, but he's definitely not hollow on the inside. Once you get him home, you'll see there's so much more to him. A lot like your guy, I imagine.

So what makes Ken the Ultimate Boyfriend? Why is he so special? Over the years I've asked myself those questions a million times. It's easy to get caught up in doubt. We even broke up briefly—I thought we should see other people. (That didn't work out so well.) Then one day it hit me: Ken's a real keeper, and I'm a pretty lucky doll to have him. Most guys would be intimidated to have a celebrity girlfriend. Not Ken—in fact, his chill attitude keeps me grounded. I don't care if he is plastic as long as he's comfortable in his own skin.

I promise, an Ultimate Boyfriend is in your future too. If you already have a guy, you're almost there. My biggest piece of advice is to do things together: put on matching clothes and go on great dates, take camping trips and go on exciting vacations—play together! Over the years Ken and I have tried all sorts of things: tennis, in-line skating, even surfing. Playtime is our number one top priority, and I'd recommend the same approach to any couple.

Ken is thoughtful, considerate, and confident, and no matter what happens he's always there for me with those strong, unbending open arms. Take it from me: why settle when you *can* have it all? Now, go out there and find yourself a Ken!

♡ Barbie™

1

how to

GET THE GIRL

All the Right Moves

Guys, take it from me. If you want to get the girl, you've gotta take certain matters into your own hands. Barbie likes to think she "hooked" me, but in reality I'm the one who put the moves on her.

Well, it was more like one move (I was a lot stiffer back in the day), but it was the right move: I made eye contact.

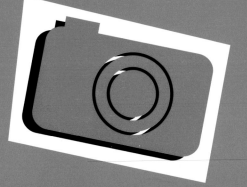

No matter which way you're looking, never lose sight of the girl of your dreams.

That's it? Yup, that's it. Eye contact is the first move in any romantic endeavor.

Now, this is important: do not stare. Girls get creeped out by it.

Some people might say that's exactly what I'm doing 100 percent of the time, but, no, I'm not staring; it's just this steady gaze thing I do. If you have this tendency too, remind yourself to turn away now and then.

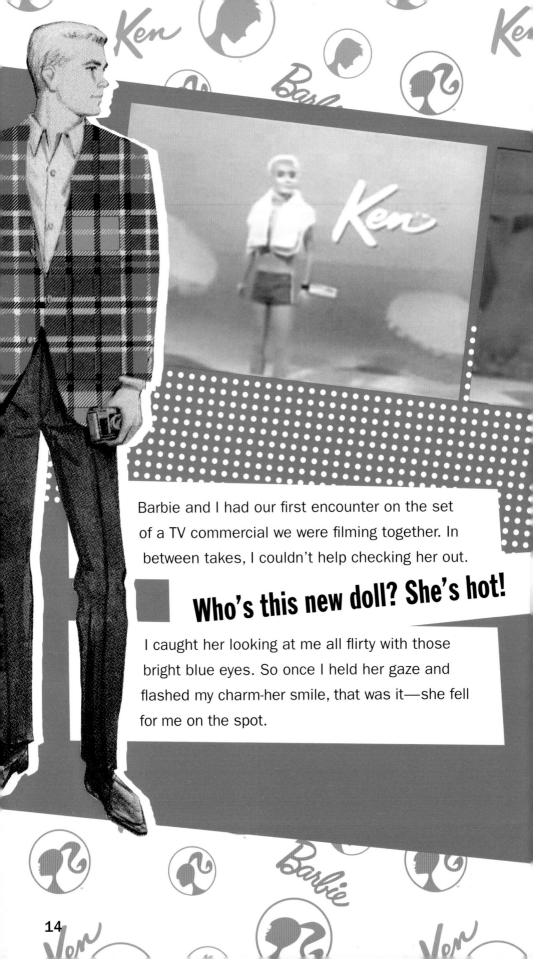

Barbie and I had our first encounter on the set of a TV commercial we were filming together. In between takes, I couldn't help checking her out.

Who's this new doll? She's hot!

I caught her looking at me all flirty with those bright blue eyes. So once I held her gaze and flashed my charm-her smile, that was it—she fell for me on the spot.

Stay classic, stay cool.

Style Points

Starting up a conversation with a girl is a victory in itself. The easiest thing is to ask what she's into: there's a good chance that you'll have something in common.

Let's face it, the most interesting girls are the ones who stay busy.

They always go for an active guy over a boring one. So, you've got her interest: you'd better keep the momentum going. Time to man up! Ask her out. I promise, if you do it with a confident smile she won't say no. Especially if you don't activate her voice chip. Just kidding.

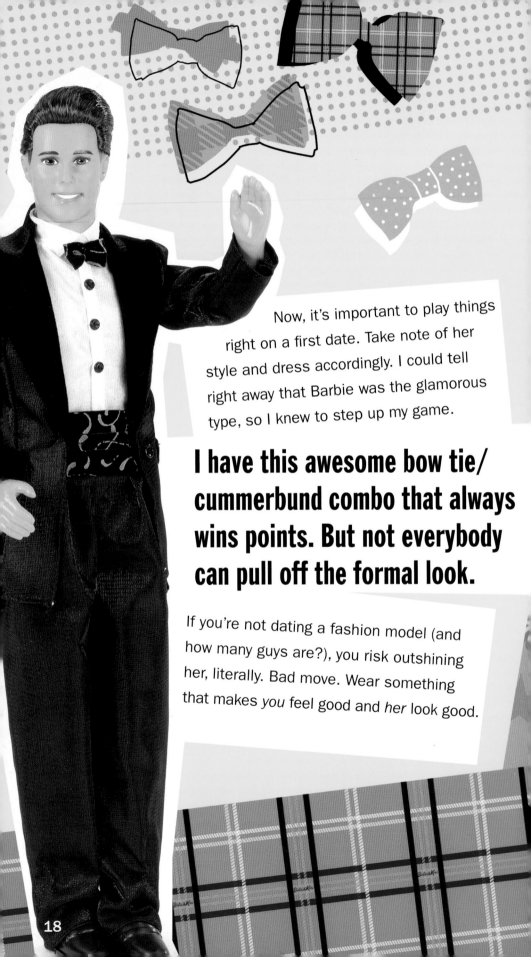

Now, it's important to play things right on a first date. Take note of her style and dress accordingly. I could tell right away that Barbie was the glamorous type, so I knew to step up my game.

I have this awesome bow tie/cummerbund combo that always wins points. But not everybody can pull off the formal look.

If you're not dating a fashion model (and how many guys are?), you risk outshining her, literally. Bad move. Wear something that makes *you* feel good and *her* look good.

Confidence never goes out of style, even if jumpsuits do.

19

Chivalry Isn't Dead

There's a time and a place for gallantry, and your first date is one of them. A man with a glamorous girlfriend has to learn the fine art of being the perfect escort.

When she says the occasion will be "totally glam," understand that it might involve sequins.

Or sparkles, or ruffles, or a color you would never imagine wearing. So prepare accordingly.

Color and accessories are important. Try matching your tie or cummerbund to her skirt.

Offer her your arm (if it bends that way), open the door for her, pull out her chair, and be interested in the event, even if you really just want to watch the game on your HD flat-screen TV.

A perfect boyfriend isn't just perfect when you're alone; he's perfect in public too.

23

Game, Set, Match!

If you look like a total cheese, well, sometimes you just have to take one for the team.

Let's say you've been dating a few weeks. Fair warning: your girl's already got big plans in mind, and I'm not talking yoga or chick flicks . . . I'm talking clothes. Matching clothes.

The mere thought of coordinating with your girl in public might put you in a cold sweat, but I'd argue there are benefits (seriously, dude).

Thing is, coordinated outfits tell the world you're a happy couple.

That makes them a great line of defense against dudes who might assume she's up for grabs. Besides, why waste your energy fighting her wishes?

Compromise is key in any relationship. I'm guessing your girlfriend has got a better eye for fashion trends than you do. Let her lead. Chances are you'll look better for it.

Nobody Says You Have to Wear an Apron

Another complexity of dating is the inevitable and often dreaded request to participate in "girly" things—things you would probably never do with your male friends. The trick to playing along is to remember that she *is* a girl after all, and doing what she wants won't make you one.

Spend some time at her place to ease into it. I was amazed to find out the kitchen is not as scary as it sounds.

I couldn't break any of Barbie's dishes if I tried!

So you're not a master chef? You can prep the salad or stir the sauce for her—this way you both get to kiss the cook. See how I'm thinking here?

The mall should also be on your radar. Yes, most men hate shopping, but if you go with her, you'll get to know what she likes. That means no more panicking before anniversaries and birthdays. Be a sport. Doing something girly today will reward you twofold later.

You're not losing your masculinity — you're earning her appreciation.

Bust a Move — Right into Her Heart

You can't talk girly activities without mentioning dancing. Whether it's your best bud's wedding or a night on the town, the dreaded dance floor *will* make an appearance at some point.

First off, guys, there's a time and a place for the Robot—it's called the '80s. And don't get me started on the fist pump. (Don't ask me to try it either. Not with these hands.)

Your best bet is to start with simple moves that look cool and can be easily accomplished even if you're rhythmically challenged. Start with the basic waltz. It only requires about four steps, but it gets her dress swirling around so much she won't notice a stiff gait. Let the music do the work, and your hips will follow.

If nothing else, stay off her toes.

Pack Her Calendar with Dream Dates

Since the very beginning of our relationship, Barbie has gotten me into a mountain of new hobbies, mostly for the simple reason that she was into them. I'm not complaining; **we always seem to be having a good time.**

I'm all tan . . . I mean man!

35

Small Gestures, Big Impact

Okay, this may come as a surprise to some of you, but girls want more than just a pretty boy toy. A little thoughtfulness goes a long way, and a well-timed gift not only shows what a great guy you are, it can also get you out of almost any jam.

Before you burn a path to the mall, let's be clear about something: size matters.

No matter what she says, your girl is going to judge your package. Make every inch count!

As gifts go, perfume never fails, especially if it comes in a fancy bottle and has something about Paris written on the label. See where I'm going with this? Small package, big wow! (Unless your head is filled with air, never tell her you bought it because it smelled good on the salesgirl.)

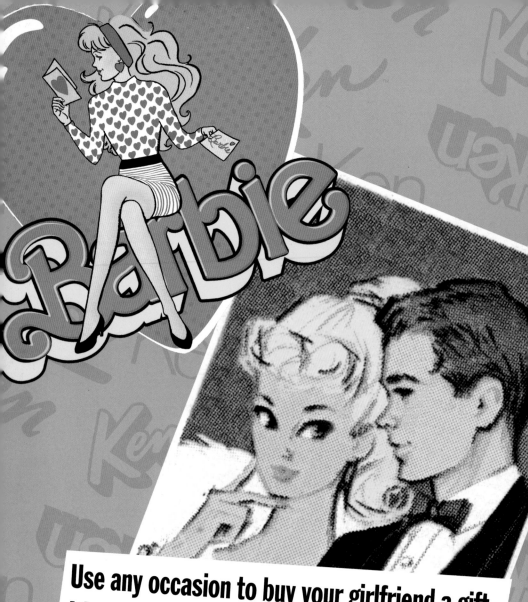

Use any occasion to buy your girlfriend a gift. It's a surefire way to make her feel special.

If you've messed up—or *she* thinks you've messed up—then a gift is an absolute must. Barbie is no pushover; sometimes flowers do the trick, but sometimes I have to lay down serious cash. I have one little problem when it comes to shopping: I don't own a wallet and my pockets are just for show. But if you're anything like me, you won't let these minor details stop you. Trust me, use your imagination, and your girl will shower you with affection.

If you accidentally tape your hand to your package while gift wrapping it, use a professional next time.

Talk Isn't Cheap

Maybe you text your friends 24/7, but don't let conversation become a dying art with your girlfriend. Engage her. Ask questions.

When she's talking, look her in the eyes and nod once in a while so she doesn't think her words are falling on deaf ears.

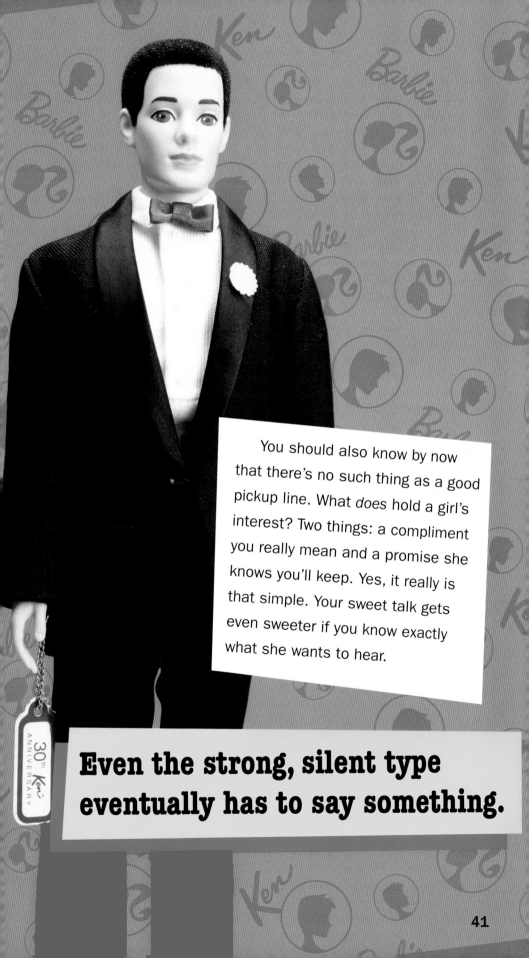

You should also know by now that there's no such thing as a good pickup line. What *does* hold a girl's interest? Two things: a compliment you really mean and a promise she knows you'll keep. Yes, it really is that simple. Your sweet talk gets even sweeter if you know exactly what she wants to hear.

Even the strong, silent type eventually has to say something.

So Fresh
and
So Clean

Speaking of sweet—let's talk odor for a minute. Not hers, yours. You knew sooner or later we would have to discuss the "g" word: grooming. I know the average guy gets weirded out anytime the topic comes up, so go ahead, shift your feet and wipe the sweat off your forehead and get over yourself. I wouldn't have to bring this up if it weren't such a point of contention in relationships.

I'm sure right now you're thinking, "Ken, how could this be a problem for you? Your hair and skin are perfect."

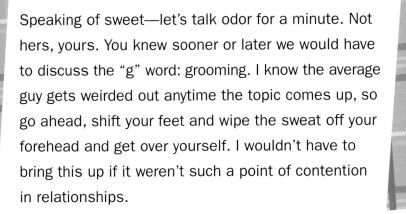

It's true, I have the kind of odor-resistant, hair-free skin that most guys will never experience. I've never broken a sweat even when traveling in extreme heat! I'm lucky like that, but I'm willing to bet you're not.

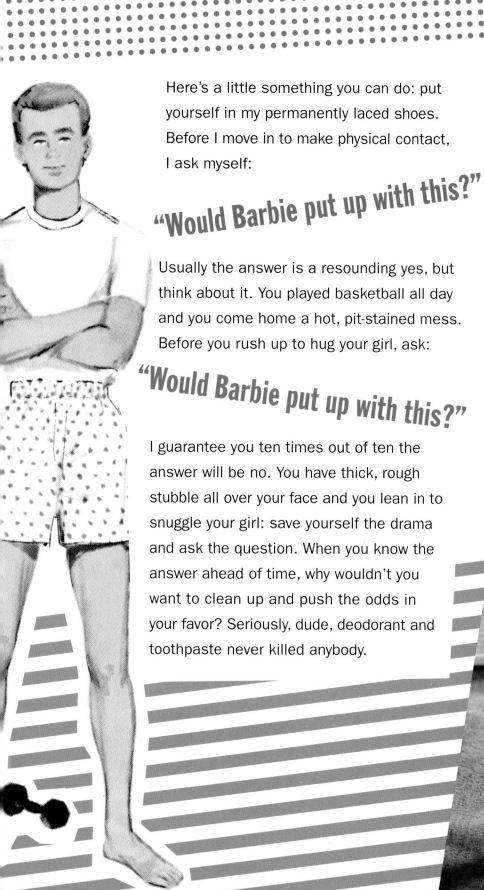

Here's a little something you can do: put yourself in my permanently laced shoes. Before I move in to make physical contact, I ask myself:

"Would Barbie put up with this?"

Usually the answer is a resounding yes, but think about it. You played basketball all day and you come home a hot, pit-stained mess. Before you rush up to hug your girl, ask:

"Would Barbie put up with this?"

I guarantee you ten times out of ten the answer will be no. You have thick, rough stubble all over your face and you lean in to snuggle your girl: save yourself the drama and ask the question. When you know the answer ahead of time, why wouldn't you want to clean up and push the odds in your favor? Seriously, dude, deodorant and toothpaste never killed anybody.

45

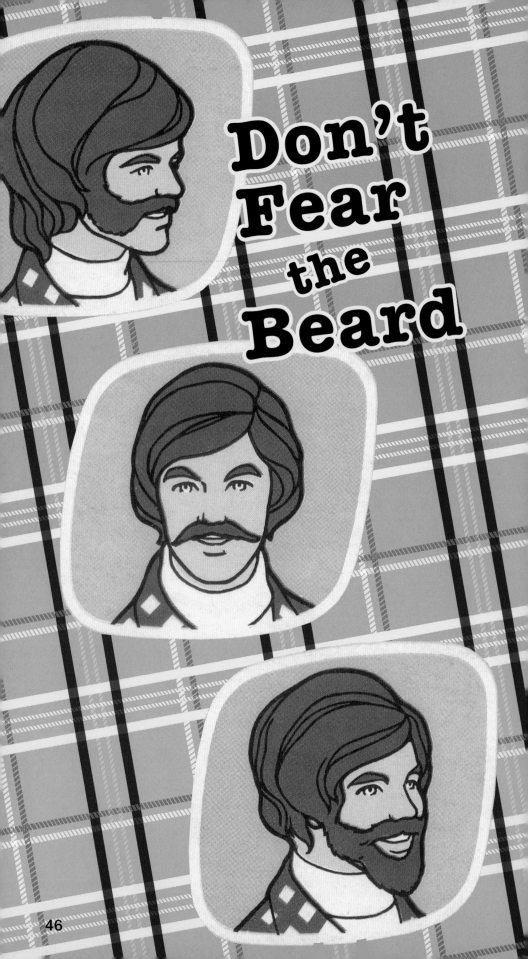

Don't Fear the Beard

I've had facial hair while dating Barbie, and she loves the way my beard and mustache seem to disappear and reappear like magic.

I just tell her I'm genetically blessed that way.
Sometimes it's good to be me.

Embrace Change

My girl is into makeovers. Herself, her car, her house . . . me. Being with Barbie, I know change is bound to happen sooner or later. If your girlfriend is like mine, you've got to jump on the makeover train when it rolls into town. You're either on the train or off the train. Don't be that guy running down the tracks.

My doll has always kept up with all the trends. When Barbie embraced change, I embraced change. When she handed me satin-trimmed gym shorts and roller skates, I grabbed my boom box and hit the rink. I learned you can't fight the disco, baby. And even with impeccably molded hair, I didn't shy away from a little facial fuzz.

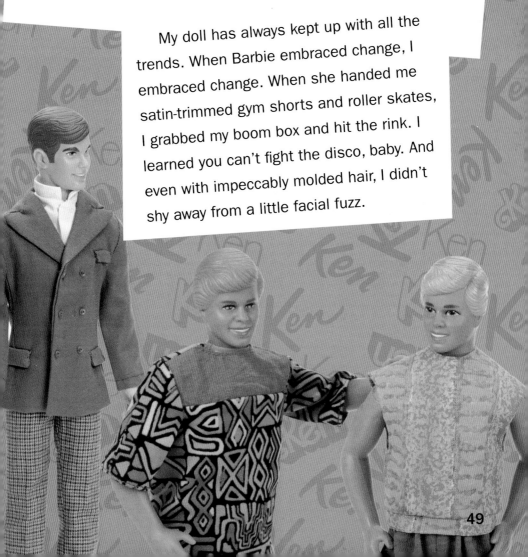

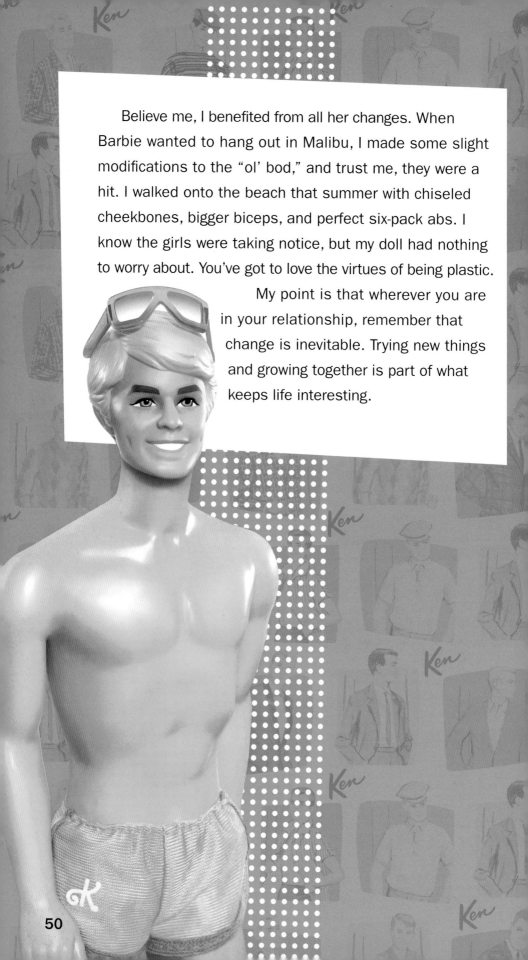

Believe me, I benefited from all her changes. When Barbie wanted to hang out in Malibu, I made some slight modifications to the "ol' bod," and trust me, they were a hit. I walked onto the beach that summer with chiseled cheekbones, bigger biceps, and perfect six-pack abs. I know the girls were taking notice, but my doll had nothing to worry about. You've got to love the virtues of being plastic.

My point is that wherever you are in your relationship, remember that change is inevitable. Trying new things and growing together is part of what keeps life interesting.

No matter how often your girl wants to reinvent herself, always remind her you love her just the way she is.

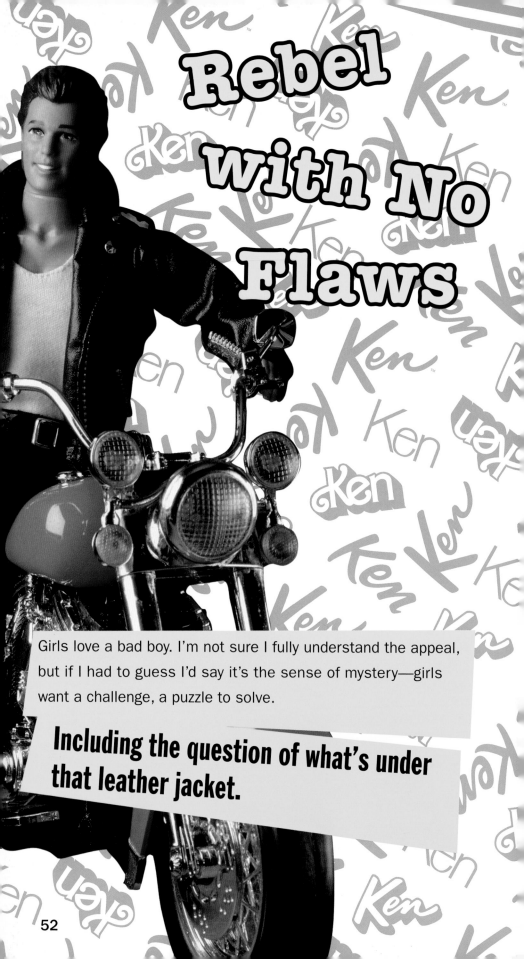

Rebel with No Flaws

Girls love a bad boy. I'm not sure I fully understand the appeal, but if I had to guess I'd say it's the sense of mystery—girls want a challenge, a puzzle to solve.

Including the question of what's under that leather jacket.

I'm not suggesting you be someone you're not, but embrace a little more of your edgy side and I bet girls will respond positively. Maybe you've always secretly wanted to own a Harley or skydive or join a rock band.

Or even get a tattoo. Listen, butterflies aren't for the faint of heart.

I was born to be wild!

Pretty Fly for a Plastic Guy

Some of my least shining moments, ironically, have been my shiniest moments....

ABS-OLUTE PERFECTION.

You're a gem!

Evenin', ma'am.

Hot 'n' hunky!

Whisk Her Away

Getting out of town together can go a long way in the romance department. Barbie loves tropical vacations, but something as simple as a long road trip gives the two of us some much-needed quality time. My doll loves to bond, so I make sure our little getaways are all about her.

He really is a doll!

For added romance, take her someplace off the grid where your cell phones don't work.

Some guys would be intimidated if they were me. Barbie has a jet, a party boat, and luxury houses in almost every major city on the planet, not to mention a killer collection of cars—and she prefers to be the one behind the wheel. But as I like to tell her, "No worries. If you fly, I'll buy!" As a good boyfriend, it's my job to make sure my doll has time to relax and be herself away from all the pressures of her many careers and black-tie galas. That's how a rock-solid relationship works: it's all about give-and-take.

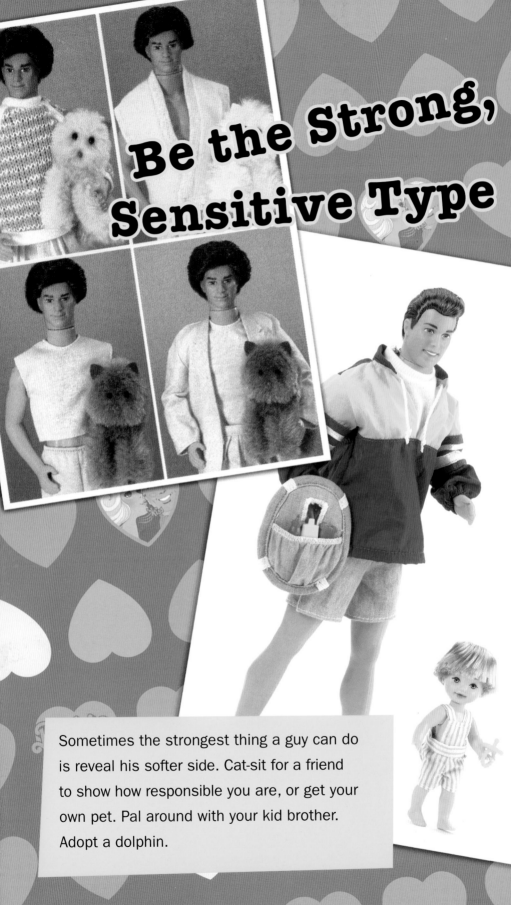

Be the Strong, Sensitive Type

Sometimes the strongest thing a guy can do is reveal his softer side. Cat-sit for a friend to show how responsible you are, or get your own pet. Pal around with your kid brother. Adopt a dolphin.

It's a well-known fact that girls find a guy with a puppy or a baby irresistible, and my doll is no exception.

Hmm ... not the monkey business I had in mind.

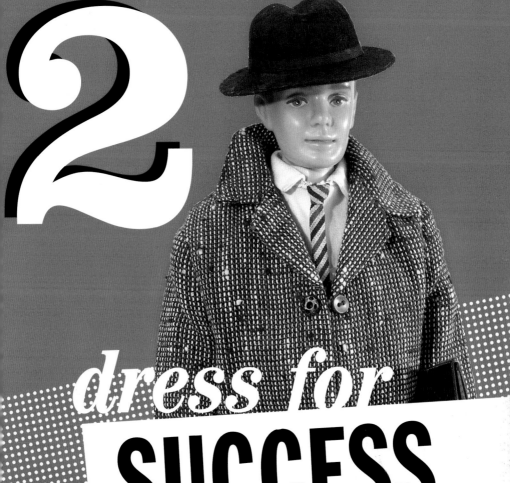

2

dress for
SUCCESS

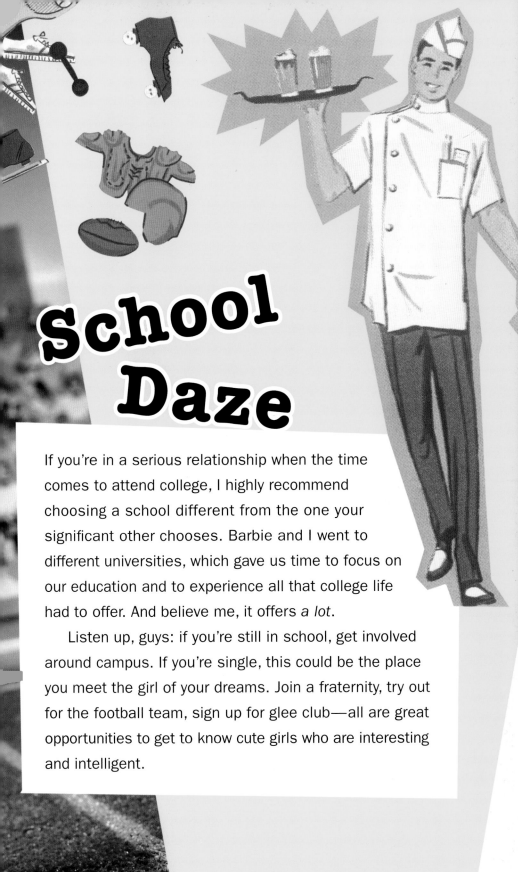

School Daze

If you're in a serious relationship when the time comes to attend college, I highly recommend choosing a school different from the one your significant other chooses. Barbie and I went to different universities, which gave us time to focus on our education and to experience all that college life had to offer. And believe me, it offers *a lot*.

Listen up, guys: if you're still in school, get involved around campus. If you're single, this could be the place you meet the girl of your dreams. Join a fraternity, try out for the football team, sign up for glee club—all are great opportunities to get to know cute girls who are interesting and intelligent.

If your girl goes to school in another town, make the weekends count: take her bowling or go for long drives in your hot rod. Get in your time behind the wheel while you can. You may never get another car, and she could end up driving *you* around!

If all you're doing is sofa surfing, you're missing out. That's why you'll never see me with a remote in hand. (That, plus the fact that my fingers don't fit around one.)

9 to 5 and Beyond

After graduation, I wanted to find a career that would not only work for me, but would also appeal to the ladies.

At the end of the day, if you have an interesting job, you'll attract interesting people.

Take me and my doll, for example—we're both very career minded. For her part, Barbie has had over a hundred impressive careers; sometimes I feel like I'm fighting to prove to the world that I have ambitions of my own.

Being this handsome, people assume I'm all about playtime, but there's more to me than that. Seriously, I'm not shallow; I'm just molded that way!

Like Barbie, I've held down just about every prestigious job there is: pilot, doctor, business-man, photographer, and even astronaut. Barbie may have run for president first, but love isn't about competition. I think I read that somewhere. Go out into the world and know what you're skilled at, know what you love, and look for ways to apply your passion.

A confident man makes the girls swoon!

My motto: I can make work look like child's play!

Business Casual

I've found that in the corporate world—as in the dating world—what you wear can make a huge difference in how you're perceived. If you've ever lost your pilot's hat before a flight, you know what I mean.

When dressing for your nine-to-five, don't forget to plan for your busy afterhours.

With the right wardrobe, it's easy to transform from day to night.

Never underestimate the power of reversible fashions. If your life calls for quick transitions, here's another option: try a dickey! This wardrobe essential is a partial shirtfront that gives you the appearance of a full collar without the actual body and sleeves of a shirt. Less bulk, more options, less effort . . .

Okay, seriously, they were huge in the '70s. Anyway.

I'm also a big fan of Velcro—way easier than buttons and zippers for putting on *and* taking off (wink, wink). Ditto elastic.

Because if there's one thing ladies love more than a man in uniform, it's a man out of uniform, if you catch my drift.

Have it both ways!

I Love the Nightlife

Don't be afraid to put yourself out there once in a while. Nighttime is the right time to shed your workweek persona entirely, from the frosted tips of your hair to the flat soles of your feet. Dress for the party.

A gold or silver medallion can take an outf from drab to rad.

BYO boom box and you'll always have the soundtrack covered.

Barbie

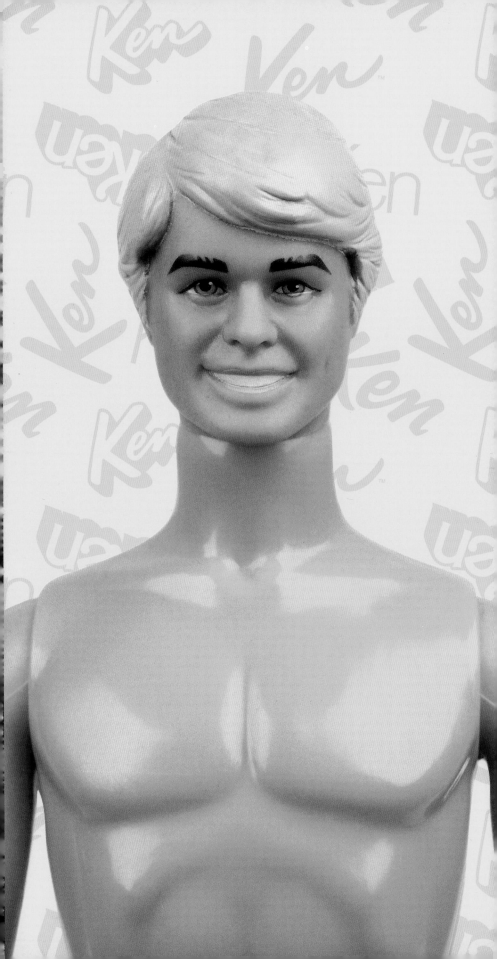

75

Share the Work, Share the Glory

XOXO
-Ken

close your eyes
and count to
KEN . . .

Working with your girlfriend can be fun, even if you have completely different personalities. Obviously, if you're the laid-back type (like me) and your girlfriend is a go-getter (like Barbie), you'll need to find the right balance. The key is appreciating each other's strengths. Barbie and I have worked on set together in a lot of movies—*Rapunzel*, *Swan Lake*, *The Princess and the Pauper*—and we've learned how to partner for great results.

While I often get to play the knight in shining armor, Barbie usually saves the day. Being there for your girlfriend is key in a relationship— even if you're in a supporting role.

79

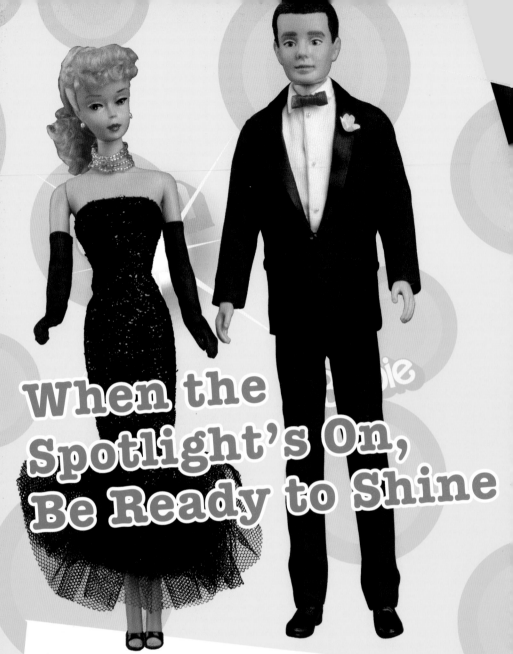

When the Spotlight's On, Be Ready to Shine

Whether or not getting attention is your thing, you've gotta play it cool when the focus shifts your way. My doll and I have walked our share of red carpets, and I can honestly say I'm not the type of guy who needs to have all eyes on me. That world of bright lights and paparazzi is so pretentious and such an epic waste of time.

Just toying with you! I'm always happy to suit up and escort Barbie down the red carpet. She may be a superstar to the world, but whenever we're together she treats me like her leading man.

Can I borrow your hairspray, Barbie?

Don't be afraid to seize your own moment in the spotlight, though. I took a chance on joining Barbie and the Rockers, and we toured all over. The outfits were another story. . . .

I guess everyone has an '80s moment they'd rather forget.

But in the end, it was all about bonding with Barbie. Moments like that can't happen if you're at home being a hermit.

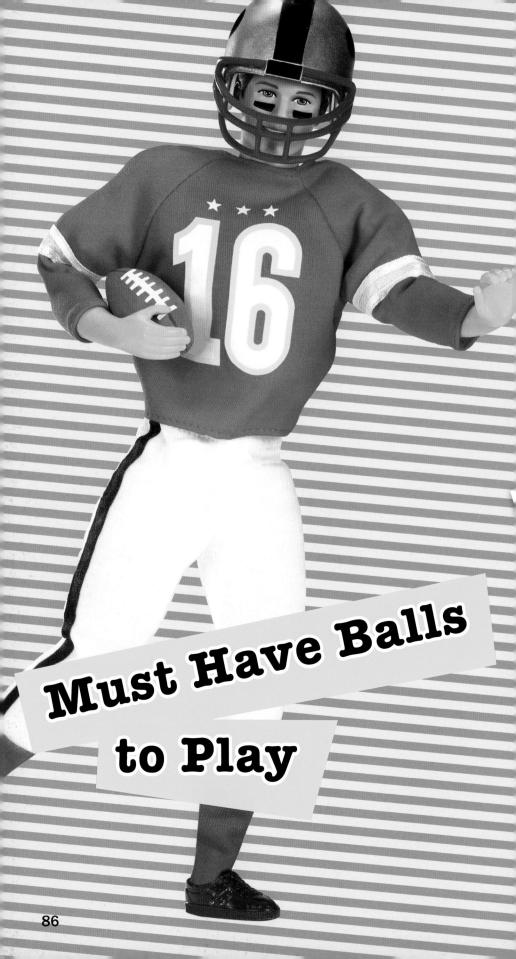

Must Have Balls to Play

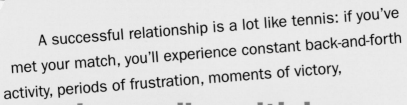

A successful relationship is a lot like tennis: if you've met your match, you'll experience constant back-and-forth activity, periods of frustration, moments of victory,

and an ending with love.

Over the years Barbie and I have had our share of relationship ups and downs. There was a time when we barely spoke to each other. She publicly dumped me and immediately started dating some loser. I mean, "*Blaine*?" Really? What kind of girly name is—sorry, getting off track.

My point is that when life throws you and your girl a curveball, you may have to sit out a few innings, but eventually you've gotta dust yourself off and get back in the game. There's nothing more attractive than a winning attitude.

Go for the . . . Bronze?

One thing that helps me feel confident is a good tan.

I'm not talking the crispy skinned, melted plastic kind of tan. Mine is strictly painted on.

Today's tan is more about safer methods like airbrushing or even using bronzer—and keeping it subtle.

Orange is a good color for swim trunks, not skin.

All those hours I've spent in Malibu surfing, waxing, swimming, saving lives, hanging out on the sand with Barbie and our friends, I've always been careful to avo[id] overexposure.

I may not sweat, but you don't want to see me reach my boiling point. Anyhoo, I've found that girls dig a guy with a tan. I'm just saying.

Chicks Dig Olympic Gold

Speaking of winning, nothing gets you into a cozy conversation with a girl quicker than whipping out a gold medal. If I may brag for a second, in 1976 I brought home the gold in not one but four events: skiing, hockey, swimming, and track.

Nobody scores like me in hockey (even though Barbie's got me beat at gymnastics). Proving you're world-class at something is one sure way to get a perfect ten from your girl. Too bad they don't give medals for surfing!

Quite a Pair

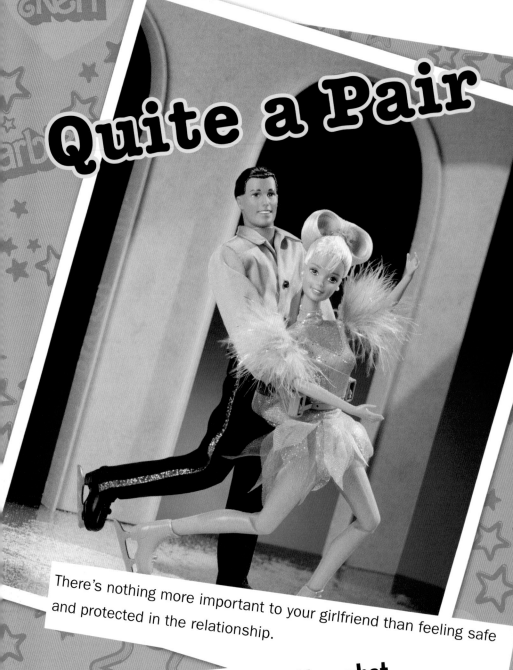

There's nothing more important to your girlfriend than feeling safe and protected in the relationship.

Let her know that no matter what, you are there for her.

A prime example: Barbie felt safe and secure in my molded hands in a daring ice dance performance. Our breathtaking jumps, spins, and lifts stole the show!

But you don't need a skating rink to prove you've got her back. A simple gesture like holding her hand as you walk down the street can work wonders.

97

Distance Training

You can never lift too many weights!

One of the most crucial factors in a close relationship is the importance of *space*. Being in love and maintaining a little distance at the same time actually go hand in hand. Being the perfect boyfriend doesn't mean being with her 24/7.

A guy needs a few of his own interests to remember that his doll isn't the only thing propping him up.

99

He's athletic.
He's all man.

ALL STAR Ken

I've always loved exercise and sports, from playing games like football with friends to solo pursuits like swimming and jogging. Physical activity helps keep you trim and terrific. Most of my go-to moves are throwbacks to the '80s: leg lifts, sit-ups, push-ups, tendon stretches—pretty much anything I can do straight legged. To help me get in the zone, I still pull out my Walkman head-phones from time to time, although most guys seem to prefer newer models.

The gym is a perfect place to get in some "me time."

Ladies Love an Athlete

Let's get physical!

Over the past few years, I've become more and more buff. (To be honest, I owe this more to the miracles of modern technology than to anything else.) Guys give me a hard time for wearing clothes that show off my body, but straight up—

if your abs were as chiseled as mine, wouldn't you do the same?

I care about my appearance and, believe me, Barbie does too.

She's already got season tickets to the gun show.

My advice is that if you really want to turn heads, you have to establish a good workout routine and stick with it.

eave the flab to the other guys; you don't need love handles to get handled lovingly.

portunity abounds: gyms are usually full of hot single girls.
rike up a conversation or offer to be a spotter. She'll love that
u're charming *and* helpful.

Already have a girlfriend? Follow my lead: keep your eyes open and say nothing.

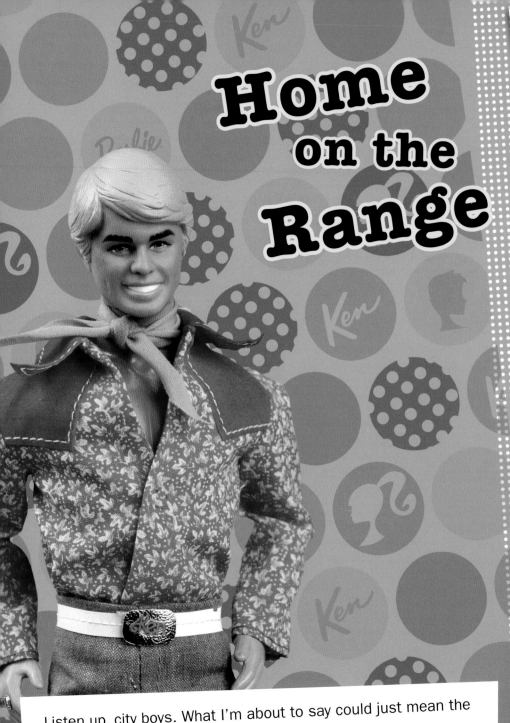

Home
on the
Range

Listen up, city boys. What I'm about to say could just mean the difference between being a boyfriend and being the Ultimate Boyfriend. I learned this from Barbie: ask your girl if she collected toy horses when she was young. If she says yes, your next move is to get in your sleek shimmer-shine sedan with power everything and drive your girl straight to the country. Do not stop until you get there.

My doll told me that girls who love horses really love cowboys.

They want a rugged, handsome cowboy to protect them from the world. Take your girl to a dude ranch. Dude, it's a place with horses!

While you're there, help feed the animals, tie something up, just show her you have what it takes to be her cowboy. Pony up for a pair of authentic cowboy boots and western jeans with stitched-on pockets and you'll have *her* eating out of your hand.

As I've said earlier, a healthy romance is about balance. I love my doll, but I need time with my dudes too. Barbie gets along with most of my friends, but let's face it . . .

there are a few rowdies I know who should never leave the toy box.

Remember, your friends are a vital support system. Mine have seen me through a crushing breakup (ahem) and every other major event in my life. Man, I wish I could give 'em a fist bump. Oh well, a pat on the back is just as good.

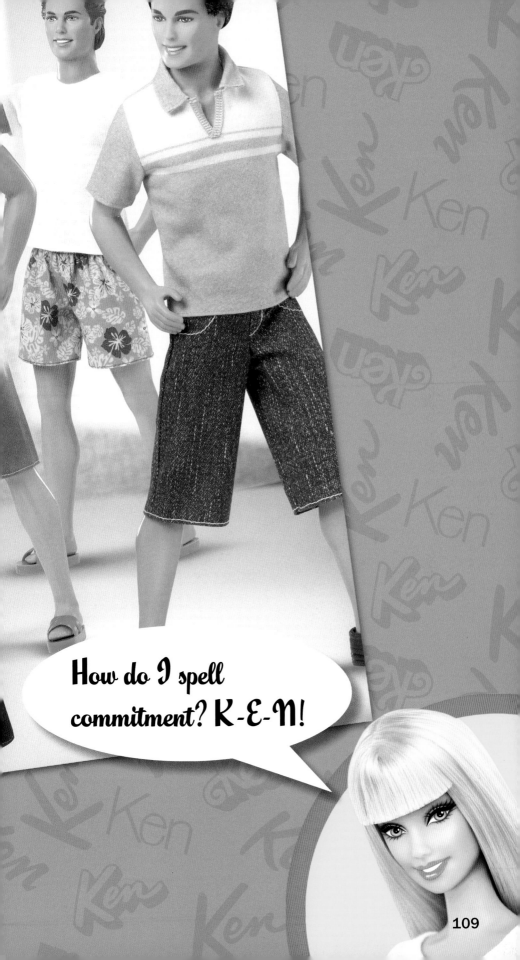

4

HOLD

your

HEAD HIGH

Cali G

Who Gets the Dream House?

Single Again!

$1.25

rlzine

Thursday, February 12, 2004

THE STORYBOOK ROMANCE COMES TO AN END FOR BARBIE AND KEN

Although Barbie has befriended some of the world's most famous celebrities, from popular boy bands to super-secret-agent spies, Ken always remained her number one sweetheart. After all, Ken has been Barbie doll's biggest supporter for more than four decades, by her side from her early career as a teen fashion model to her recent turn as movie starlet. Their relationship was so revered that other successful celebrity pairings were often dubbed Barbie and Ken.

Although their future is yet to be set in cement, one thing is for certain—Barbie and Ken will always remain the best of friends.

113

Surviving a Breakup

Breakups are tough. It hurt like h-e-double hockey sticks when Barbie left me for that loser Blaine. I felt lost and alone for a minute—until I realized Barbie did me a favor. When you and your girlfriend hit a bumpy patch, let me tell you, fellas, that may be your lucky day.

No guy wants to see his doll on the arm of some other man.

Still, you've got to go on living and live well. Once she realizes she's with a loser, she'll start looking at the dude who's acting like a winner: you. Then you, my friend, are on to step two of breakups: making up. If you've heard any breakup-to-make-up songs you know what I'm getting at. Wink, wink!

There Are Other Dolls in the Toy Aisle

Dolls may change and are subject to availability.

I'm a NEW MAN!

Breakups can lead to breakthroughs. Dude, get over it. Breaking up with your doll is tough and even worse when the whole world is watching, but you've got to man up and move on. After Barbie and I split, I hibernated in my man cave. You can only do this for so long. I kept reading about how much fun Barbie was having with that loser. I knew it was high time for me to get off the couch and get my plastic you-know-what in gear.

There were tons of dolls in the aisle. One of them would be happy to meet a guy like me.

Happily Ever After?

Barbie™ & Ken™

It happens to all of us: the inevitable run-in with the ex. And when it does, you'd better be ready to grab the bull by the horns. I knew that Barbie and I were slated to appear together at the *Toy Story 3* premiere; what I didn't expect was that the moment we stepped on to the red carpet together, arm in stiffly angled arm . . .

all of those old feelings were about to hit me, hard. I knew I had to win her back.

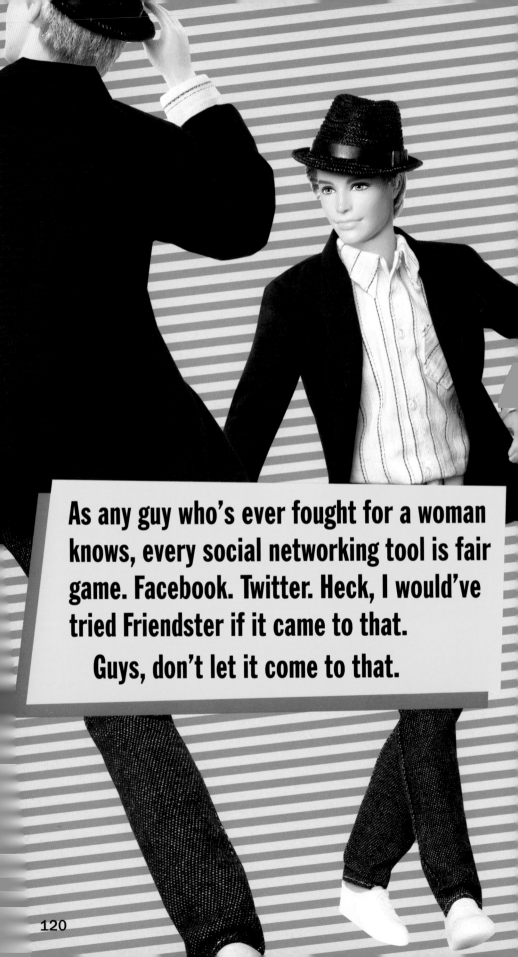

As any guy who's ever fought for a woman knows, every social networking tool is fair game. Facebook. Twitter. Heck, I would've tried Friendster if it came to that.

Guys, don't let it come to that.

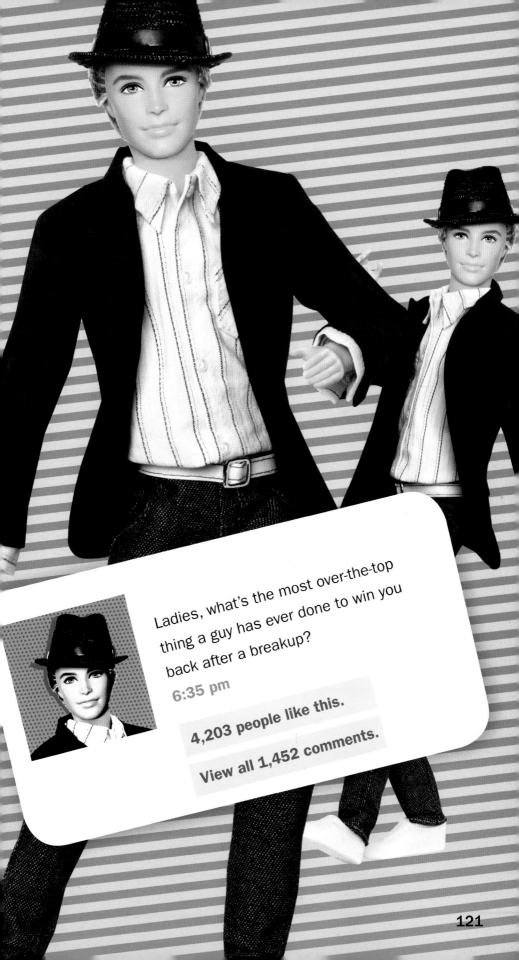

Ladies, what's the most over-the-top thing a guy has ever done to win you back after a breakup?

6:35 pm

4,203 people like this.

View all 1,452 comments.

Lessons Learned

Big goals call for even bigger gestures. (Yes, even bigger than Twitter.) That's what led me to take my biggest leap yet in my quest to win Barbie back: I wrote down every single tip I could think of for becoming the perfect boyfriend. And then I found a publisher to compile them—in this very book.

I can't promise they'll work for everyone. They haven't worked every single time for me.

But if you can take anything from my story, maybe it's the comfort in knowing that even the most unshakeable guy can be shaken up by love.

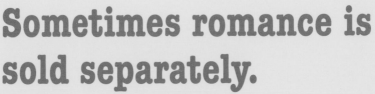

Sometimes romance is sold separately.

123

Final Thoughts

I get a little embarrassed when people refer to me as the Ultimate Boyfriend. Talk about pressure. I didn't set out to be the Ultimate Boyfriend; that persona simply evolved. One day I asked myself, "Ken, if you were a big-name product, what would you do to enhance your image?" I started thinking branding, public relations, bigger package, and other strategic stuff. When your girlfriend is a world-class icon and everyone's watching every little thing you do, you have to be on point and show them your best game.

Then again, Barbie makes it easy for me to be the Ultimate Boyfriend. She knows I would never toy with her emotions; she's truly the only doll for me. Most of the time I just show up and she does all the work, which makes me more than happy to do things with and for her.

We've been through a lot together, but in the end it's only made us better. Dude, fifty years—fifty years!—and I can still say my doll is my best friend. After all this time, we're still having a blast.

So, guys, if you really want to be the Ultimate Boyfriend like me, I have one simple rule of thumb:

Treat your girlfriend like she's Barbie and everyone will be happy.

— Ken™

Thanks, You're a Doll!

It takes passion, dedication, and knowledge of all things Ken to make over our leading man into the Ultimate Date. (Groovy doesn't happen overnight!) Special kudos to Ken's living dolls.

Vicki Jaeger

Monica Okazaki

Kathleen Warner

Julia Phelps

Darren Sander

Emily Kelly

Tanya Mann

Sarah Quesenberry

Judy Tsuno

Jim Holmes

Brad Armistead

Matt Repicky

Bill Greening

and our special Ken-sultant,
Eleanor Oliver

About the Author

Jef Beck is the owner of *Keeping Ken*, a Ken doll collector resource Web site that chronicles Ken doll's history. He also owns the largest Ken doll and Ken doll fashion collection in the United States. Originally from Independence, Missouri, and currently residing in Cedar Rapids, Iowa, he has written several feature articles for *Barbie Bazaar* magazine. In 2010, Jef was credited for helping with the depiction of the Ken doll fashions that appeared in the Disney/Pixar film *Toy Story 3*.

Acknowledgments

This book would not have been written without the hard work and patience of becker&mayer! editors Kjersti Egerdahl and Amy Wideman.

Many thanks are also extended to Mattel, who envisioned this project and shared archival imagery for this book. I am especially thankful and respectful of Mattel for allowing me many opportunities over the years to express my personal passion for the Ken doll brand.

Additionally, what makes this book unique are the people who "get" me. To my partner, Jim, who deals with my Ken fandom. To my parents, Don and Claudette, who let me play with Ken as a child, and my sisters, Brenda and Missy, who allowed me to permanently "borrow" their Ken dolls a few days after the excitement of Christmas 1970 was over. Thanks for cutting your little brother some slack. To my Ken collector friends Dwane, Jack, Mike, Dorinda, and Norita, who supported my passion for Ken in the beginning . . . and to the rest of you who love Ken as much as I do.

And finally, to my best friend. Thank you, Sandi, for your unwavering confidence, guidance, and pure love. You will always be the Barbie to my Ken!